GOTHIC KITCHEN

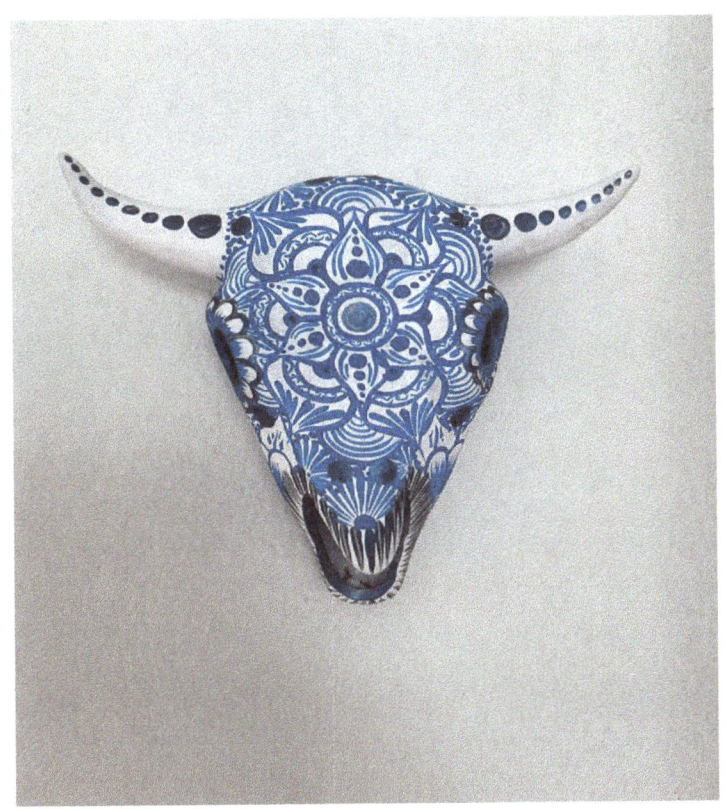

Poetry & Kitchen Musings

Lauren Ferry

TABLE OF CONTENTS

Eating The Mind

Stories To Tell At The Table

Roots Of The Rotten

Food For Thought

Eating Cake

For the love of God, pay your cooks!

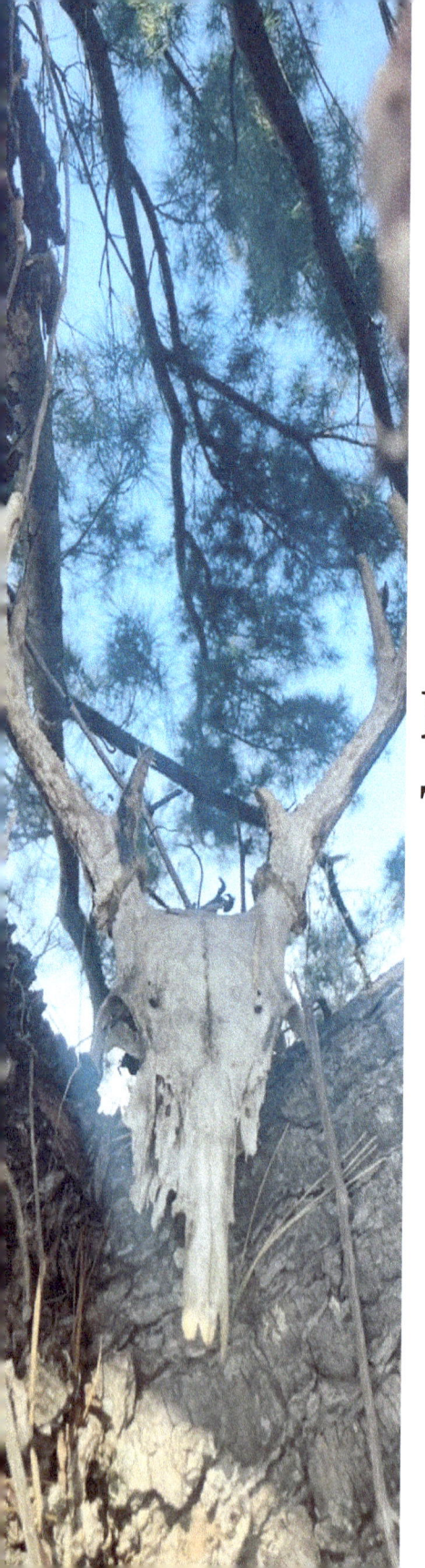

01
EATING
THE MIND

THE VULTURE

HE picks it.
That meaty,
Dirty,

Dead-

Boned, ripped
Carcass.
With nothing

Dead-

Eyes.
He picks it.
Breathes, survives
Today.

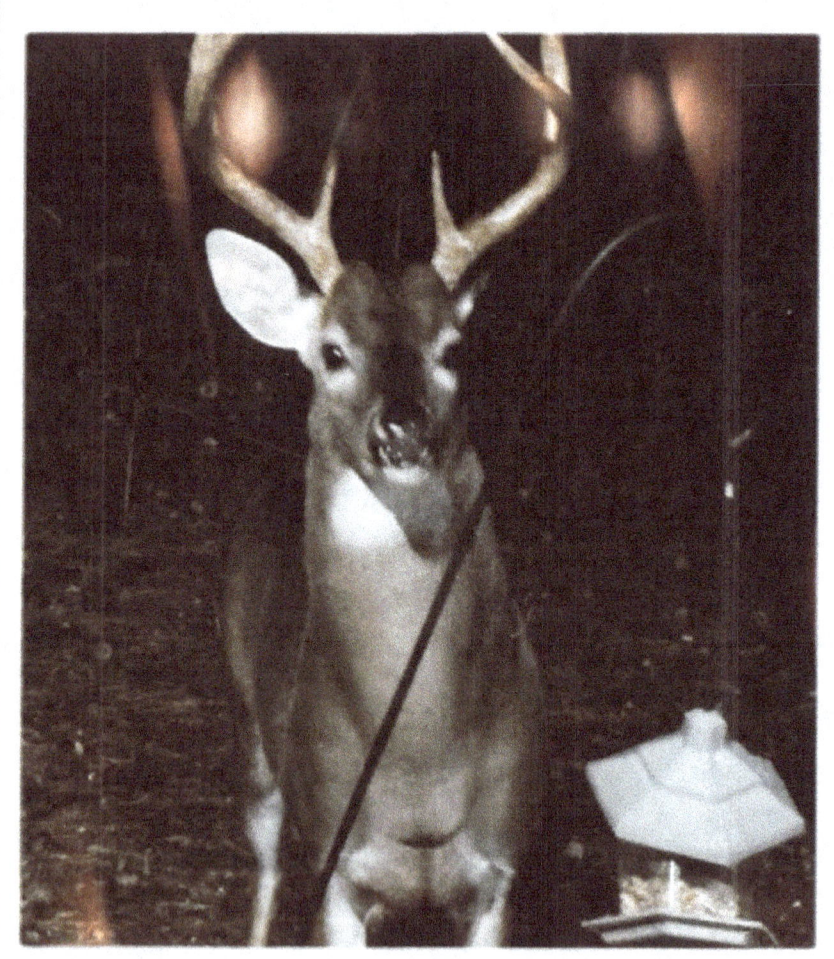

Hilton Head Island, South Carolina

SCRUBBING

SHE scrubbed

The blood of the carcass

Out

Of the threads

Of the apron

But,

You could still smell it.

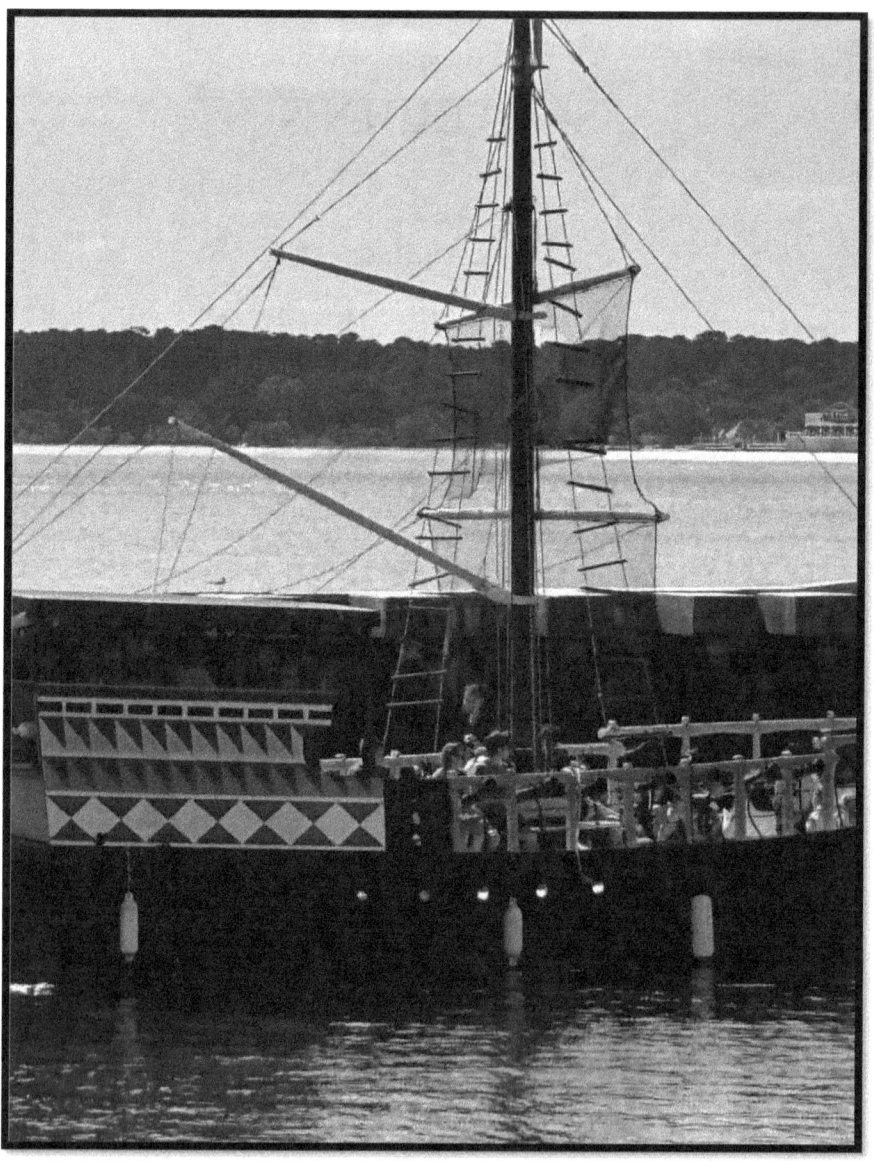

Hilton Head Island, South Carolina

CATACLYSMIC WAVES

SHIP
Wrecked
And sailed
Under,
Drowning
Deep.
Cataclysmic waves,
Too treacherous
To count sheep.
Fog strangles,
Chilling hooks.
Dream of shores
And Penelope's looks.
Diverge from her
Suitors,
A blasphemous fate.
Swim Home
Or your bleeding love
Will be
Too damn late.

Lauren Ferry

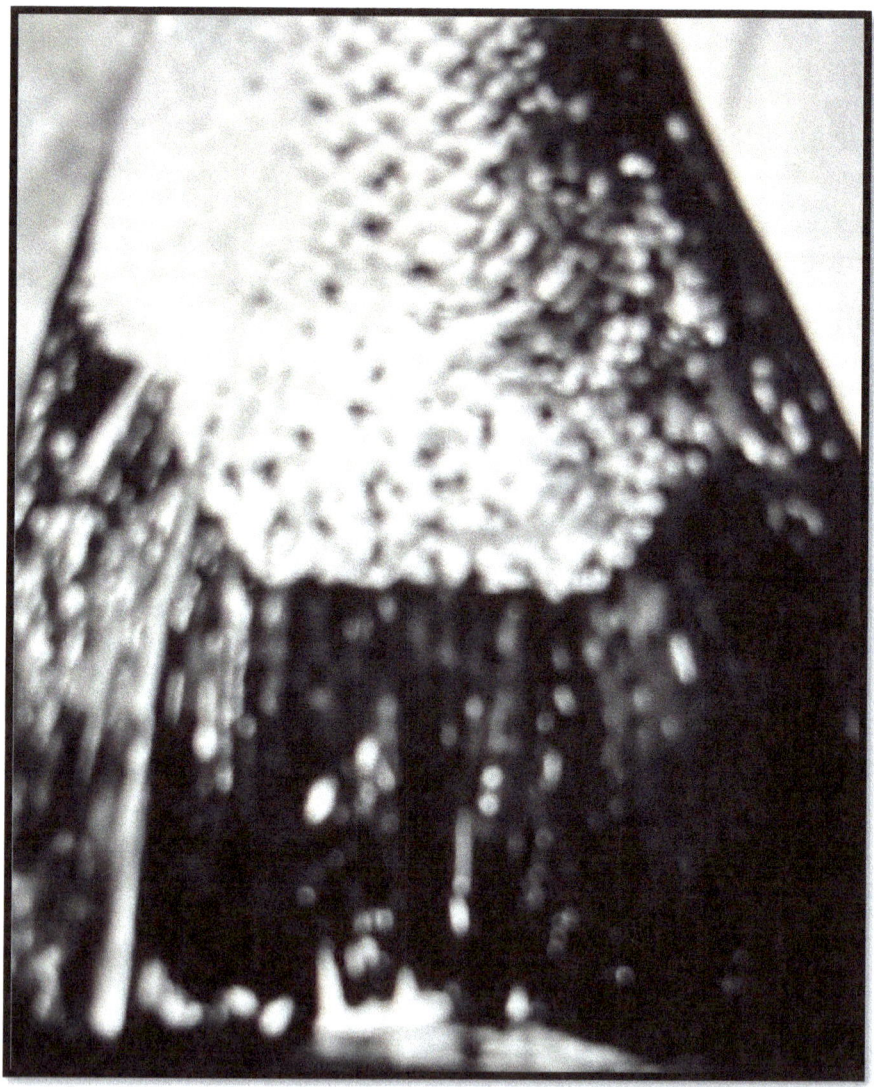

AD HOC

Grabbing a hand
Full
Of salt,
He slathered it,
Smeared it
All over
That silk flesh
Of salmon.
Among other things
In a cure
Of Ad Hoc,
She
Was perfect.

Lauren Ferry

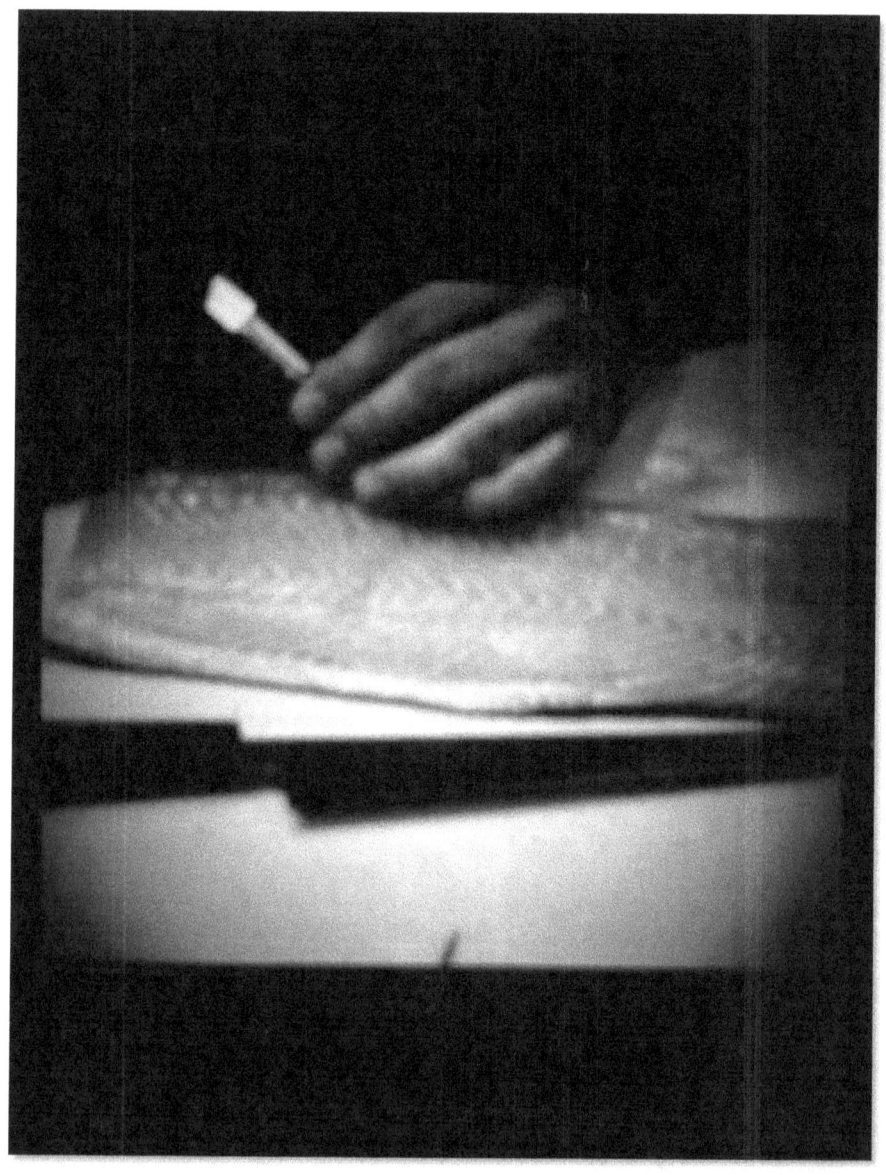

THERAPY

The fish

Is laid

and ready.

Delicately,

Pin bones

Are tweezed,

A therapeutic Repetition.

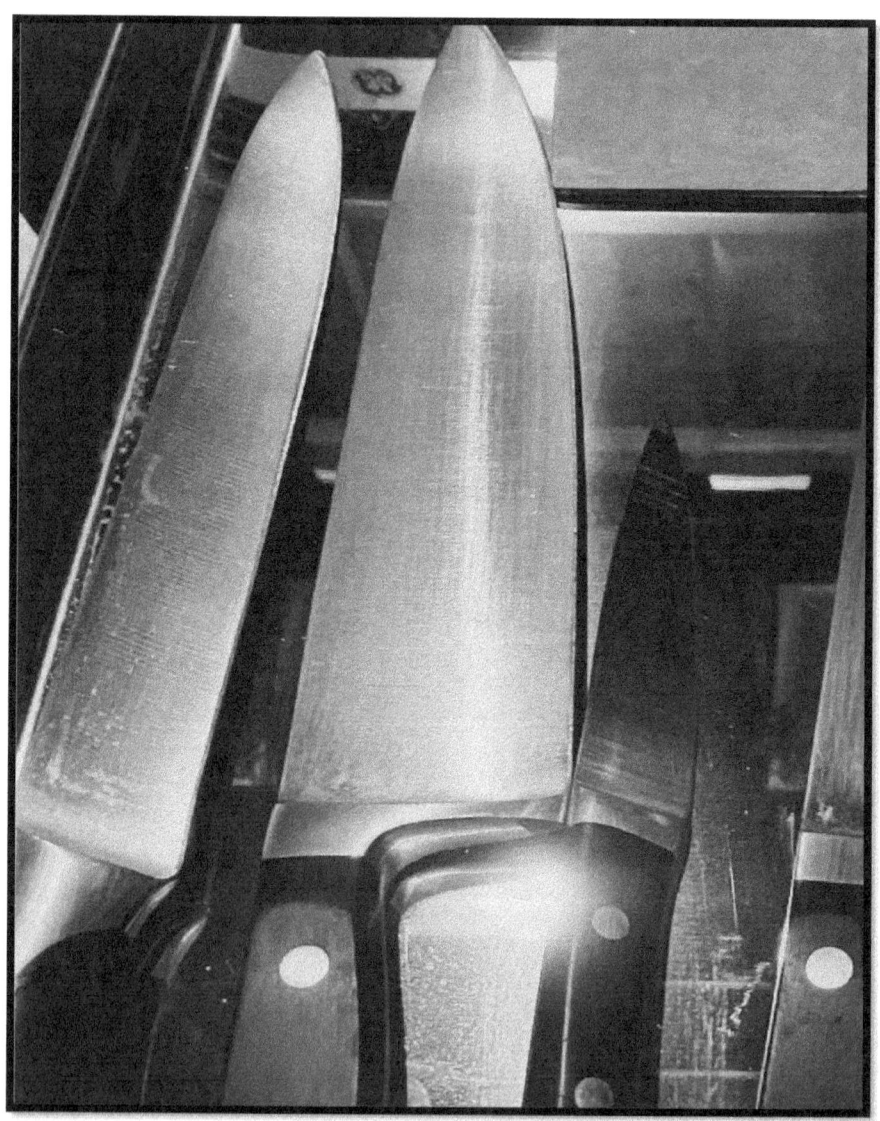

LIKE BUTTER

The German

Steel

Is wet

Stone

Sharp.

I trim

The fat

Cap

Of the Coulotte

Like Butter.

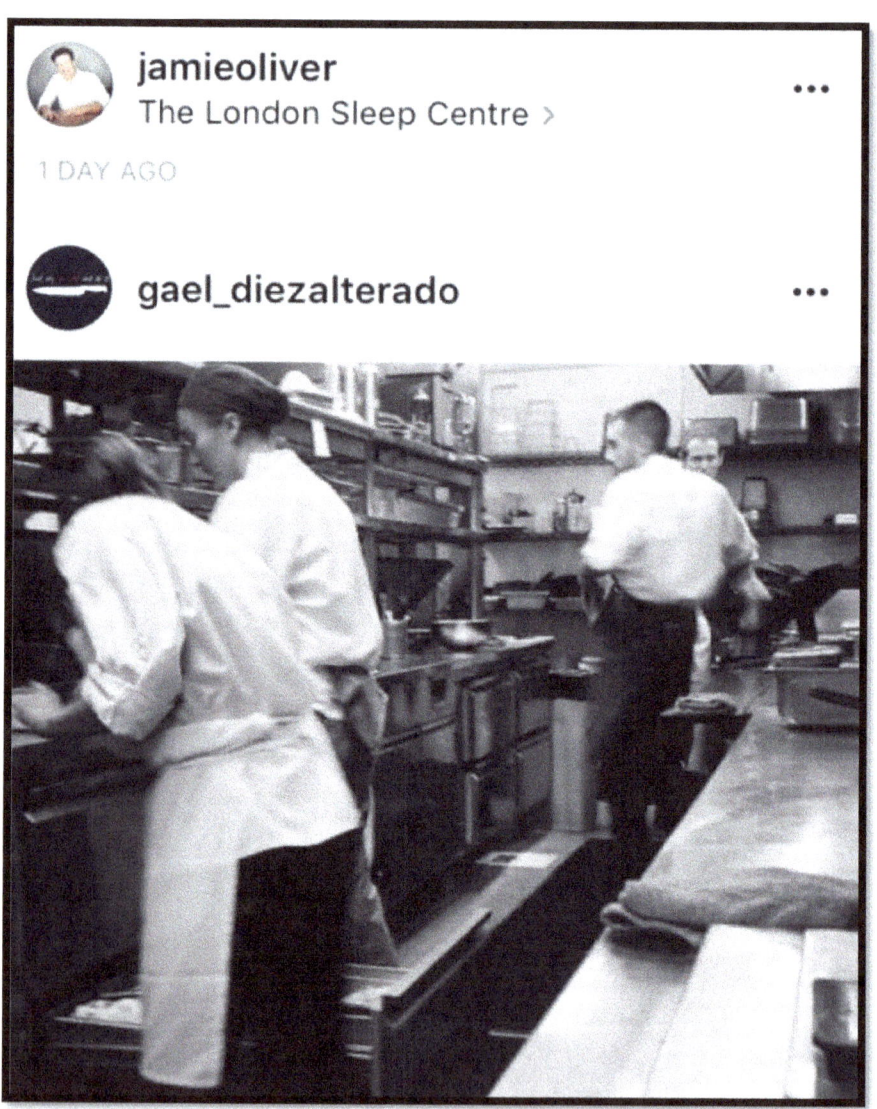

Solage, Calistoga, California
One Michelin Star 2014

GUILTY

She looked through her

Glass.

A bowl

Of super vision

A realization;

The suffocating

Kind

With more salt to taste

In the mouth.

When will she be
Off the hook?

Lauren Ferry

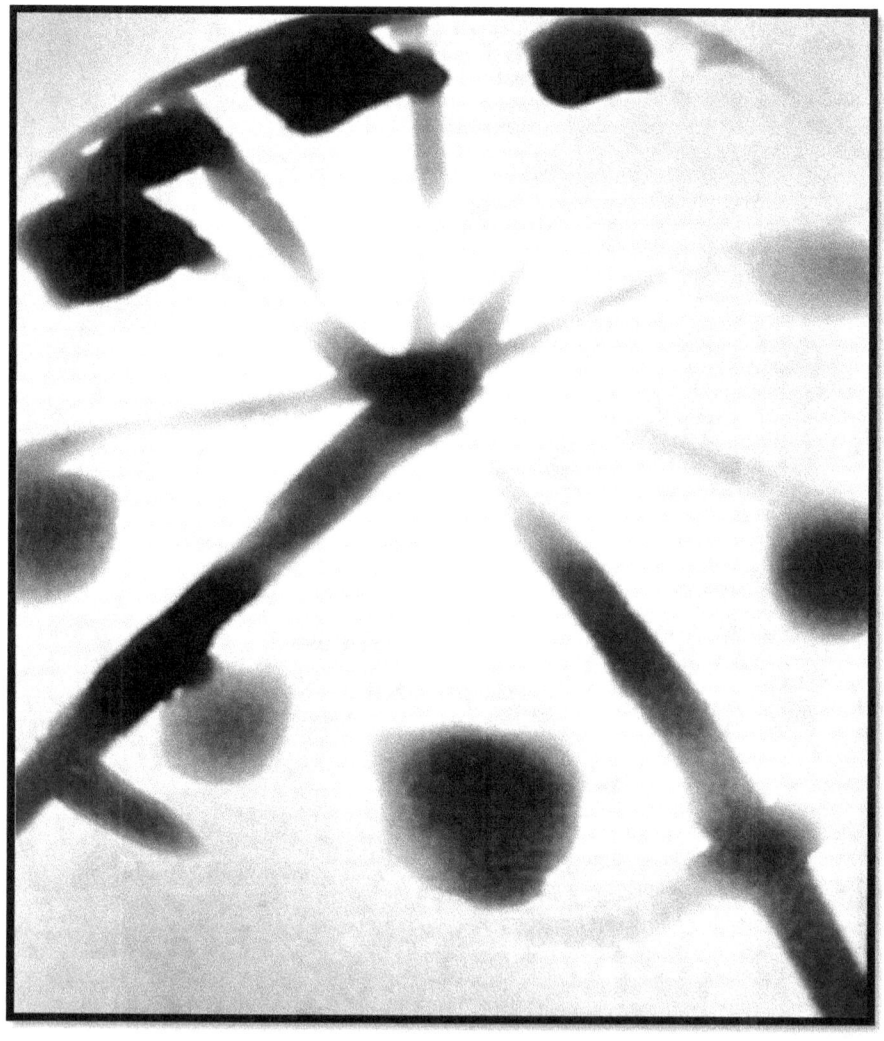

THE BRAIN

A tilt-a-whirl

On fire

With no

Hose

To put it

Out.

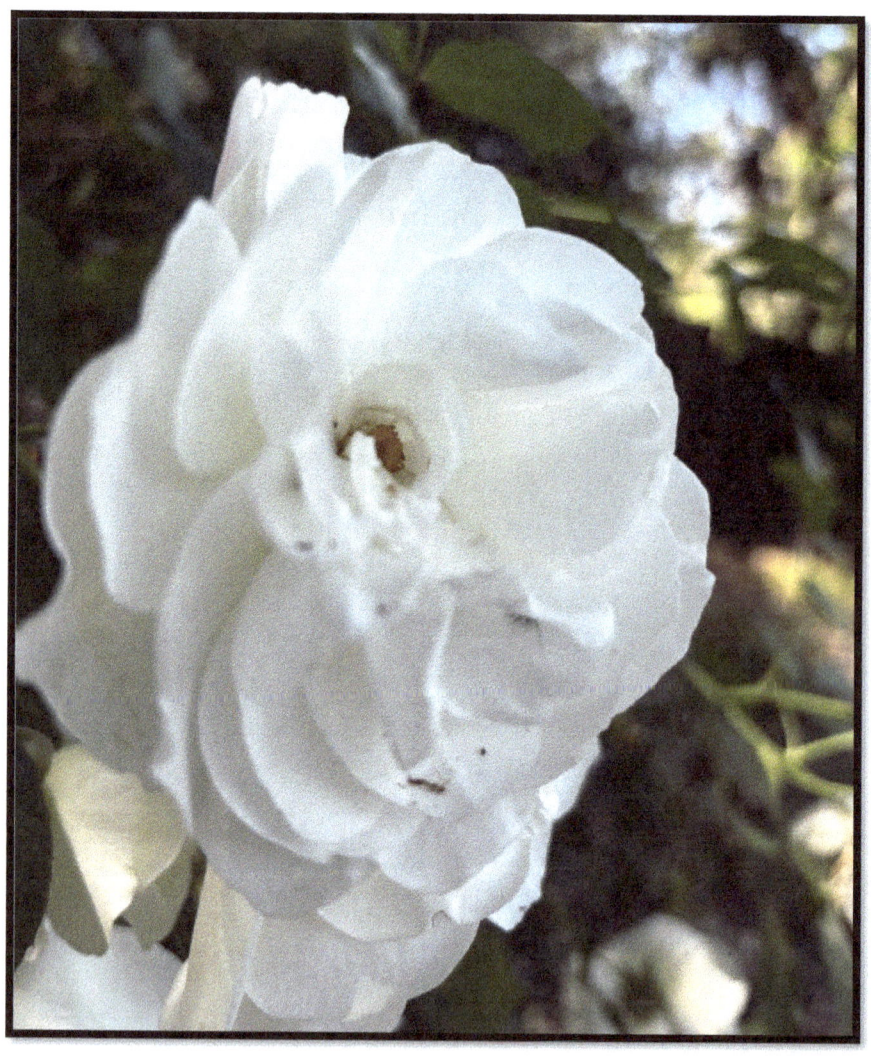

THE HEART

It escapes, the blood
But leaves
The heart
Pounding in
Morbid
Speed.
In piercing
Pain,
The heart
Cannot decipher
Between heart
Attack or panic.

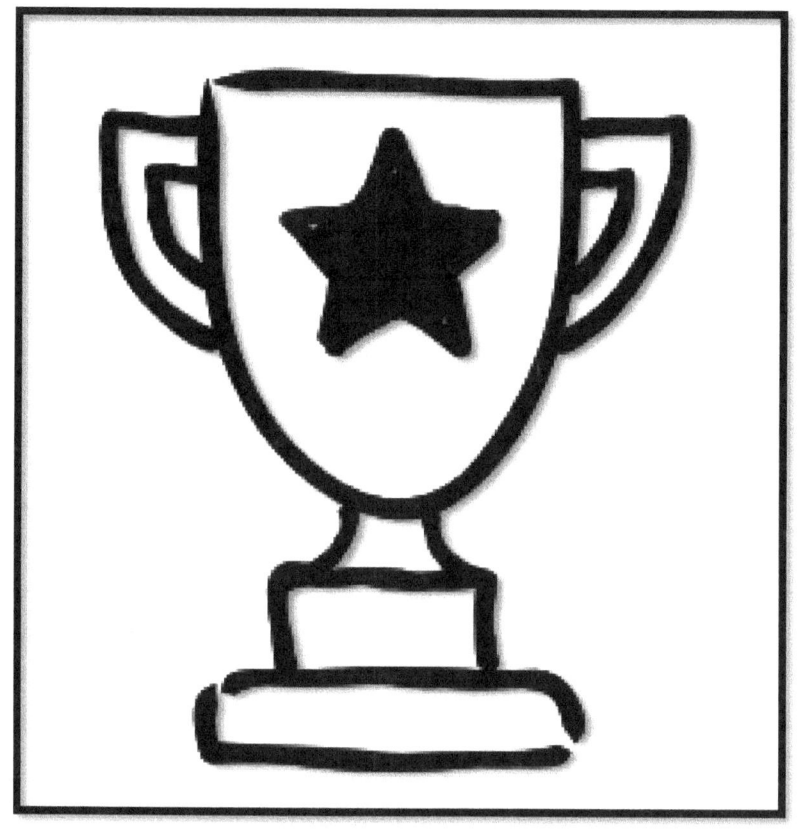

THE GAME

HE ENTERED
Hungry
And full
Of madness.
The kind
A dog has
Foaming-
Brilliant
Scary
Ready
to play.
All bones taken,
Eaten.
How easy A win, Cujo!

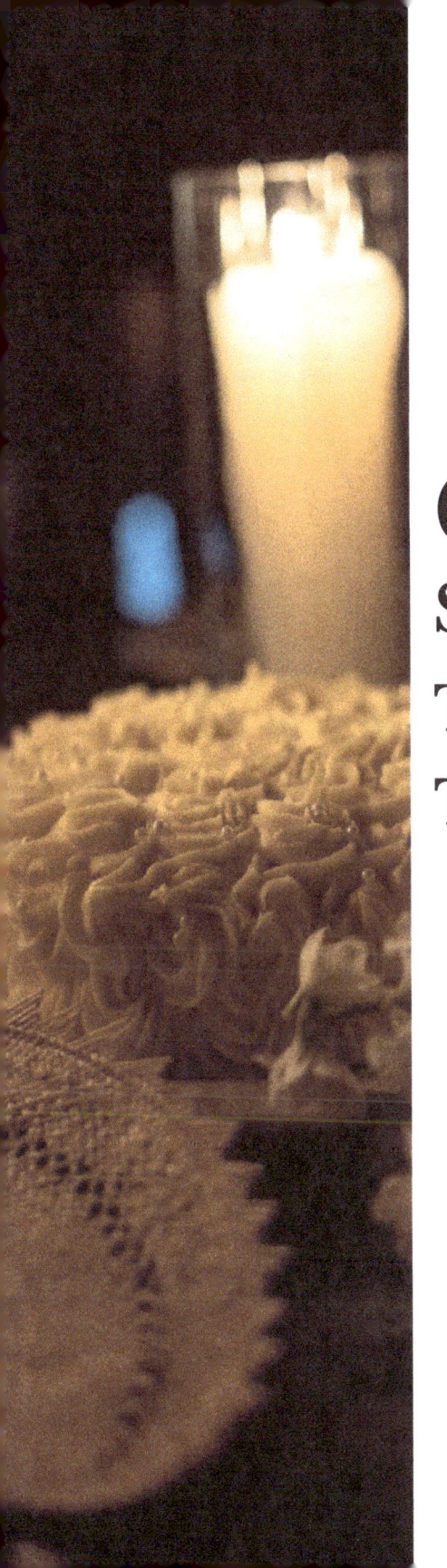

02
STORIES TO TELL AT THE TABLE

Lauren Ferry

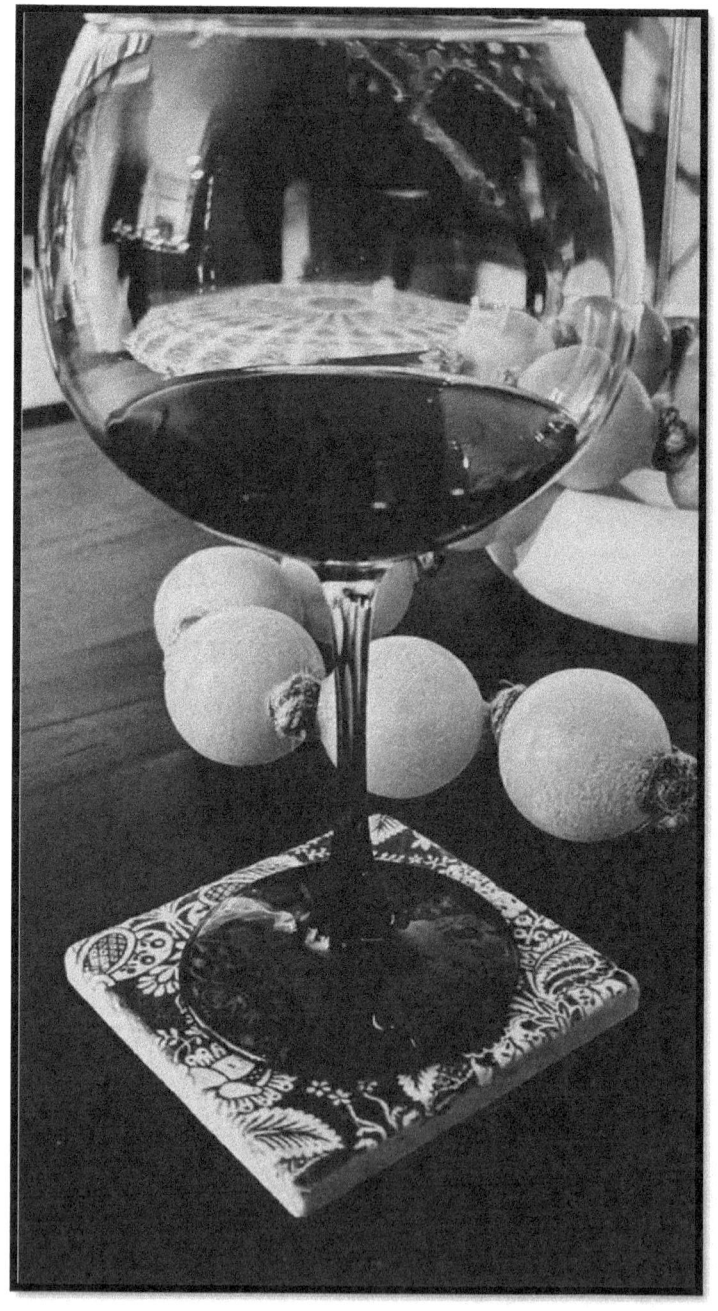

SOMETHING PECULIAR

One crimson glass
Is poured
At one
Bone chilling
Table for two.
Bread is buttered,
A casual slather
Awaiting the waiter.
Pates, frog legs, snails,
How sweet a spread!
Something peculiar.
Something pale and frail.
Or them-
Looking straight from the veil.
Candlelight paves a slither,
Red wetness
From the kitchen door.
One cup is set.
He claims thickened
With roux.
One question-
What the hell is in this stew?

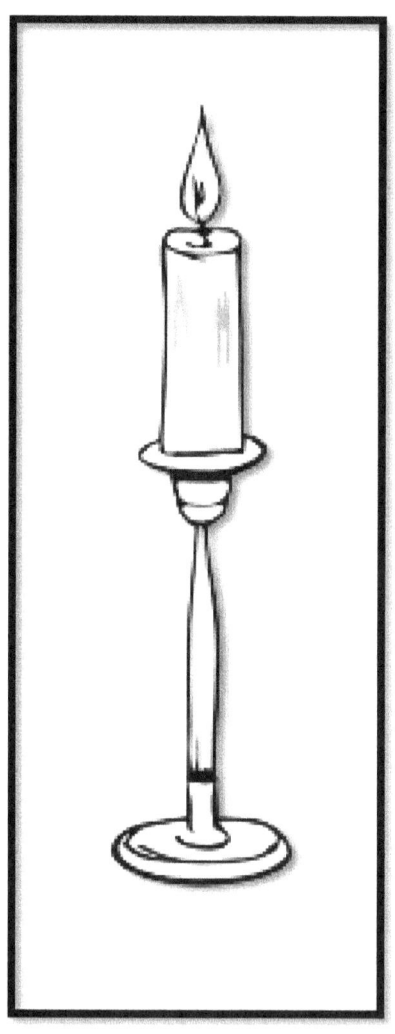

DINNER WITH A PRINCE

A room,
      Sterile.
A table,
      Trestle.
He sits phlegmatic,
      You sit erratic.
He steers.
      You veer.
Pretty plates,
      Six courses.
Aphrodisiacs,
      Chef's portions.
His entree's untouched,
      You notice.
Cabs drank,
      Drunk.
This castle, cold,
      Colder.
He smiles.
Teeth
      Pearly
Sharp.
I shouldn't have come.
Welcome to Transylvania after dark...

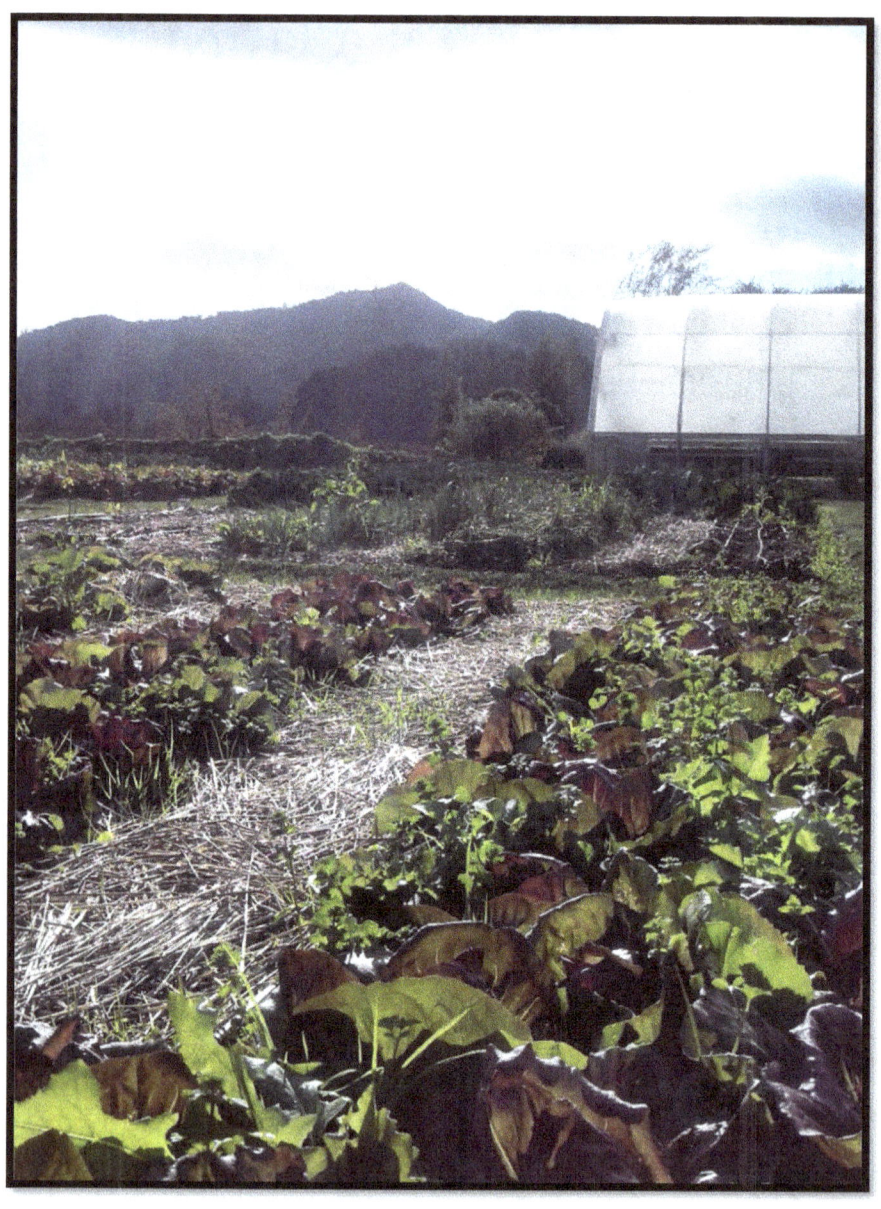

The French Laundry
Garden ~ Yountville, California

TO MEAT A MAN

HIS pleasantries

Were muddied

By the tangled smells

Of others.

Soured perfumes.

Overcooked sulfured eggs and
meats and

Swine,

A formaldehyde blend

For the snout.

And when he rambled,

He offered

One hoof.

It was less

Of an offering

And all

For the taking

That gluttonous evening.

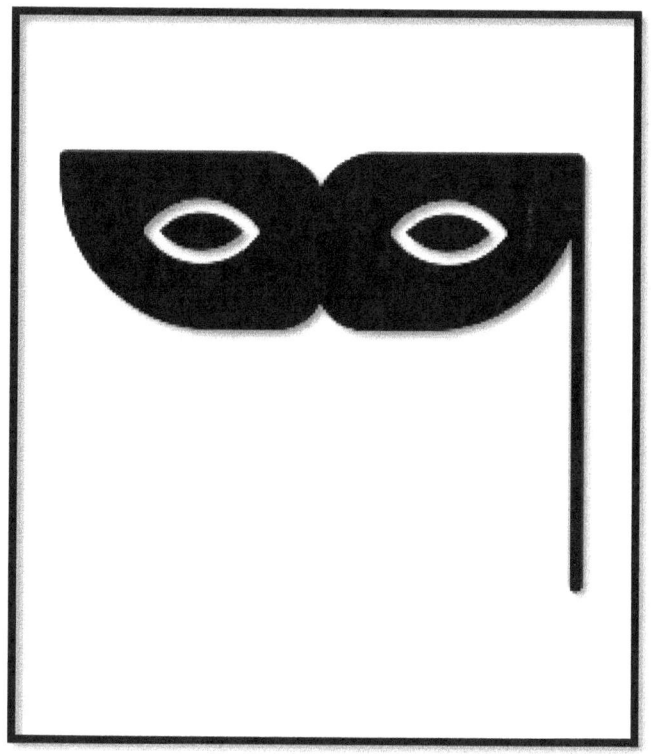

MASQUERADE BALL

Masquerades
And glittered things.
Secret lips
With pretty names.
Many fingers, all no rings.
Midnight chimes,
A dance of late.
Eyes
Dead and gone,
Can't escape.
What a grand eve
Of seduction.
Too much green fairy,
A theatrical production.
Perhaps a villain
Is deduced,
And I
Your puppet.
This is just a classical
Thou Out Whodunnit.

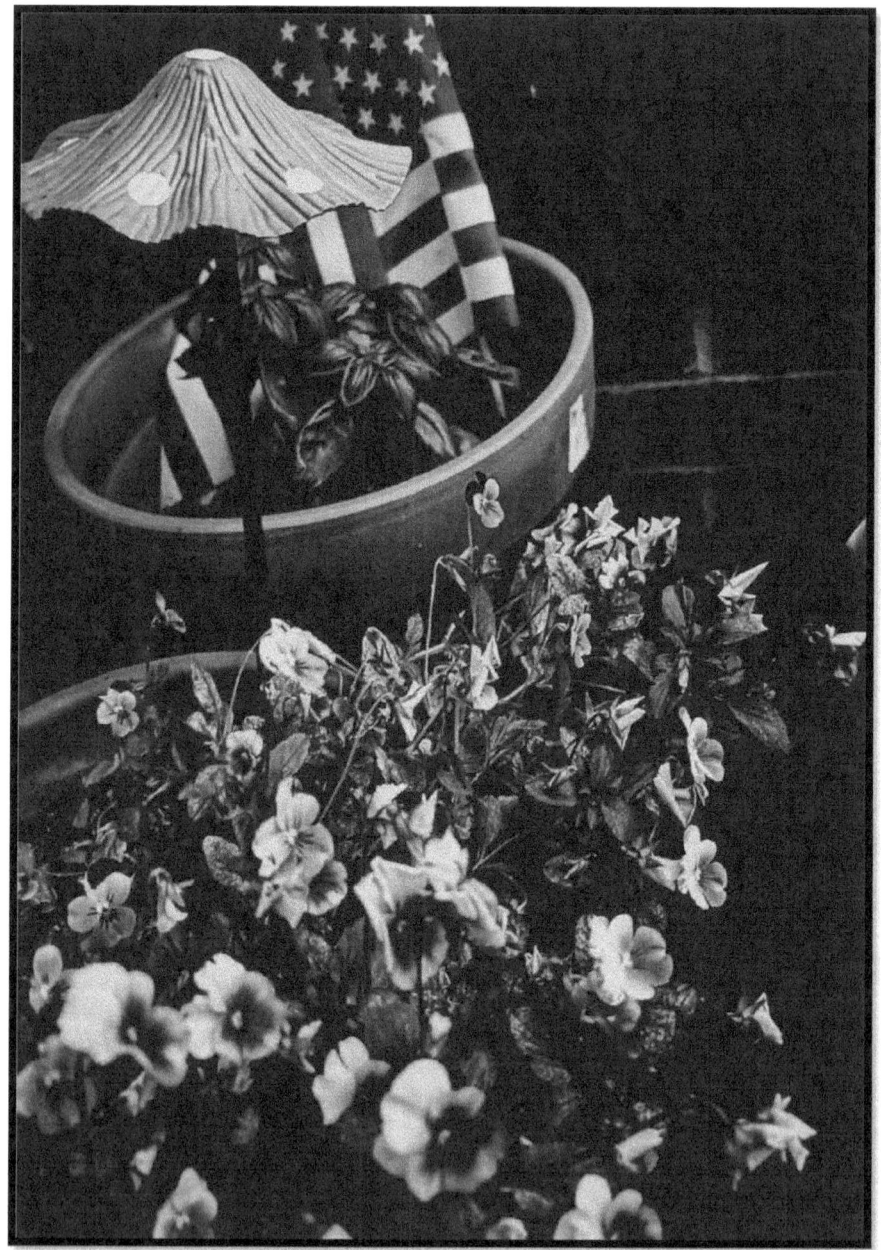

COFFEE TABLE

The porch,

The rocking,

The Minute Maid.

Southwest summer, slow.

I sit.

I rock.

I watch.

The kids run in

Imagination.

Across the road,

She weeds.

And weeds furious.

Her succulents, strategic.

You can see them now. And her pot

Of basil, well

I reckon you'd mistake

For a small tree.

It would surprise me

None

If you found

John Keats on her coffee table.

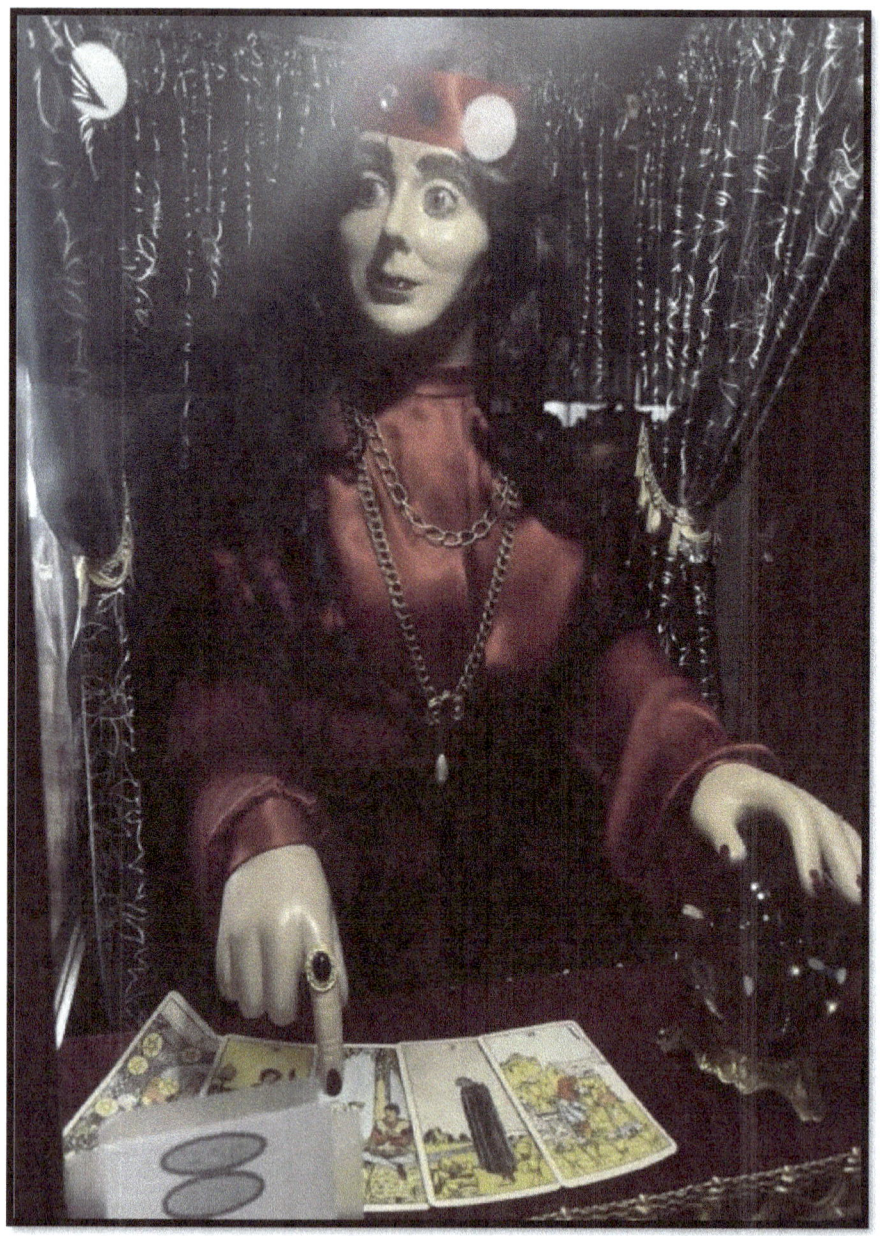

TEN OF SWORDS

BOURBON STREET, 1946.
One stalemate soul.
One card, no spread-
Ten of Swords.
"I see the Highest Count
Lost, stolen
Breath
Blood, death,"
She said.
Six eternal years
And one day,
But let's rewind it say
Five:
Enter the United States alive.
This Pearl
Harbors no sparkling fate-
Only tears, good mate.
"Where to next, Ms. Shirl?"
I said.
"Honey, I'm sorry.
You've been shot
Down,
Dead,"
Mr. Major Ted.

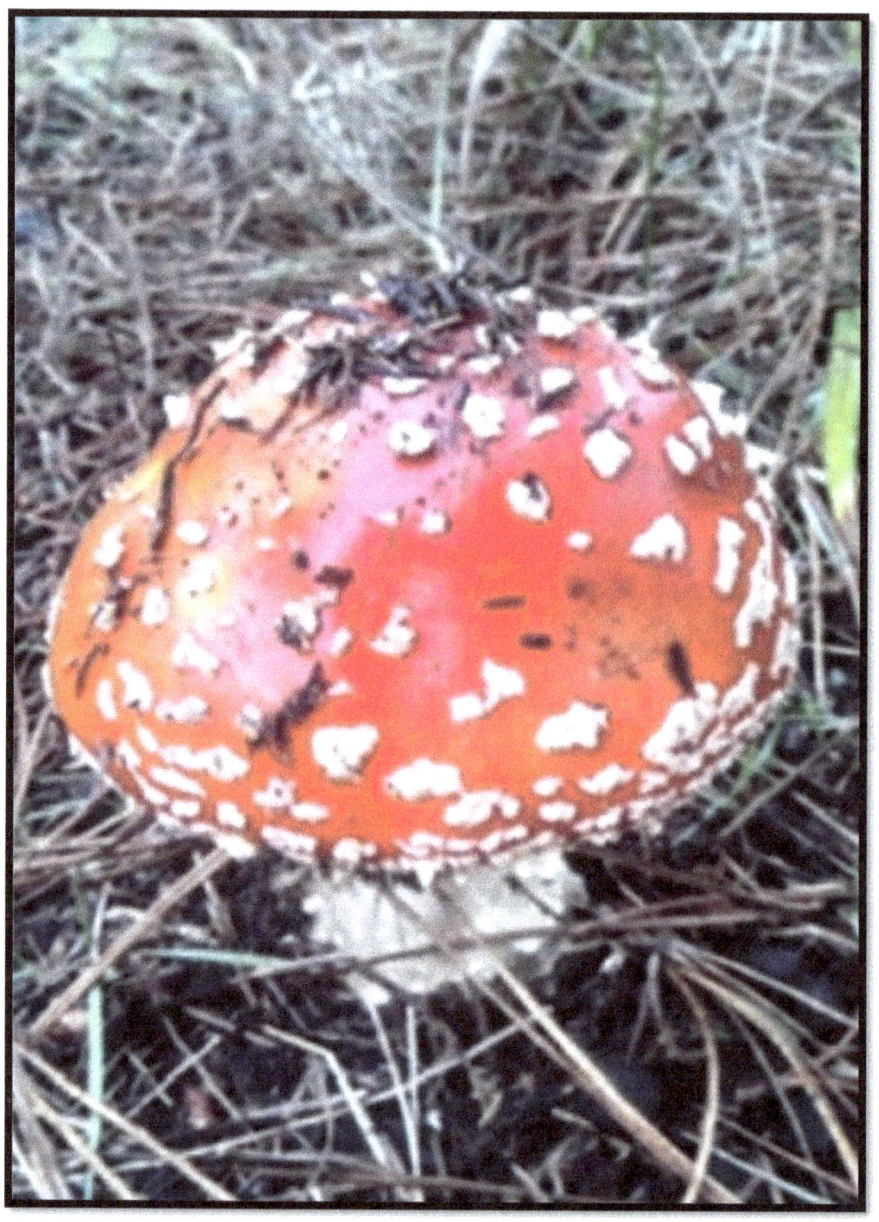

Point Reyes, California
Mushroom hunting

TWISTED TEA IN THE PETRIFIED FOREST

Into the Redwoods,

Burnt and dead.

Farm to table,

A basket of stale bread.

Teacups chipped,

Unstable and red.

Must be grandma's China,

An unfunctional spread.

Bloody hell,

Tetanus outdated!

Chaotic creatures

And strange things plated.
Clocks set backwards

Making timeless mistakes.

Nothing truly matters.

There are holes in this cake!

Pass the whiskey.

Drown this mad scene.

Might as well serve cheap Lipton

To the goddamn queen!

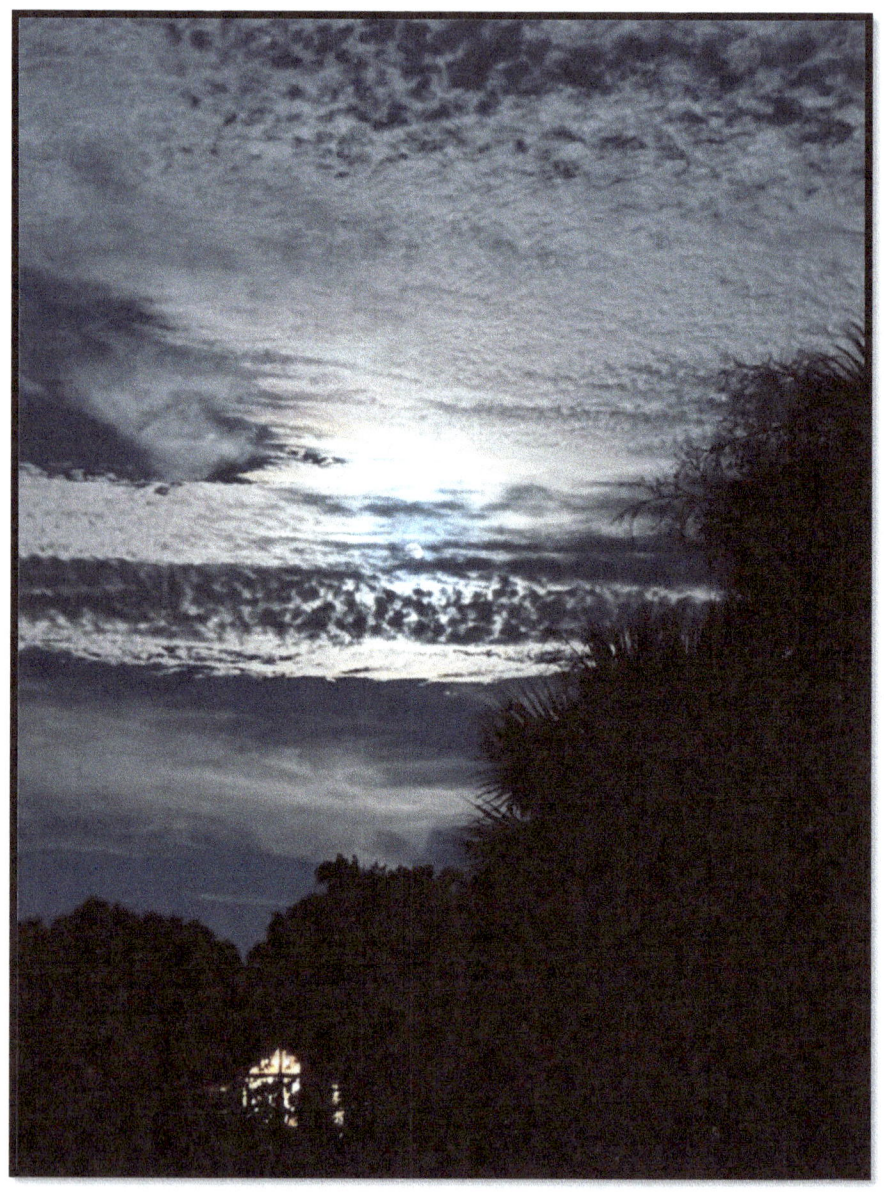

Hilton Head Island, South Carolina

ORBS OF THE NIGHT

Hovering delicately

In darkness

She glows,

Soft and swift.

A dainty

Illumination

For creatures

Of the Night.

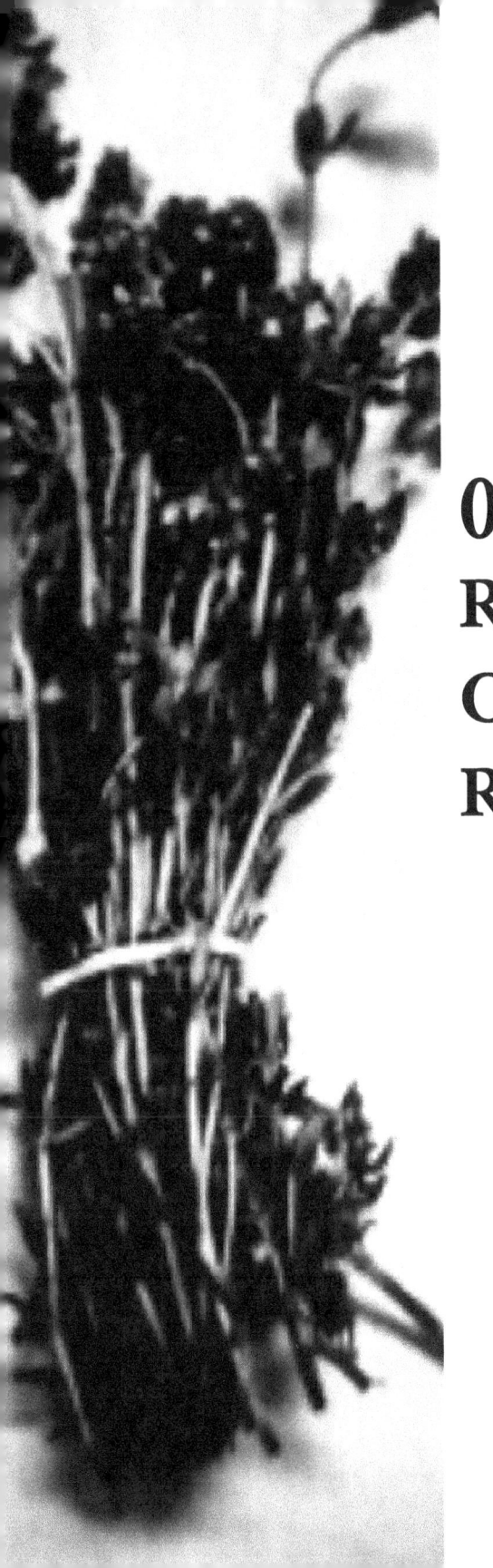

03
ROOTS
OF THE
ROTTEN

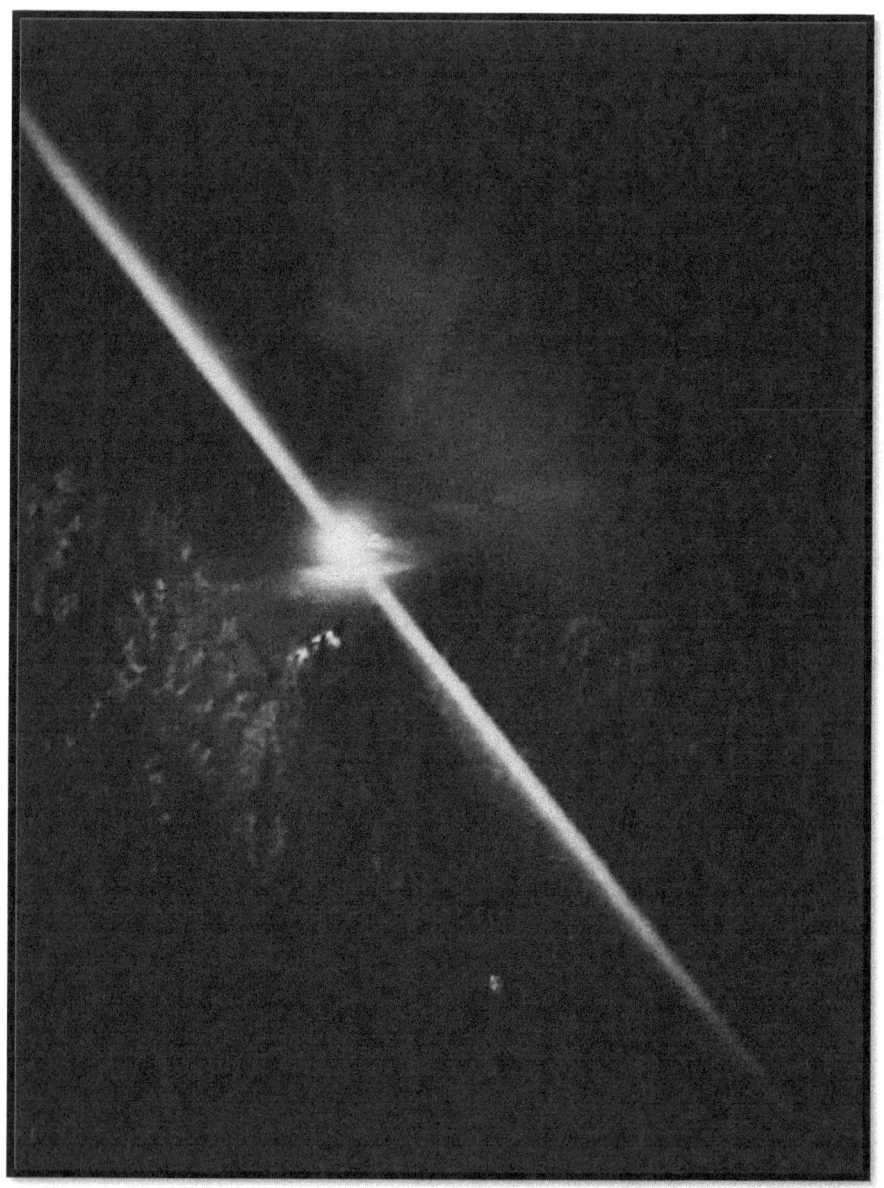

SPACE

I cannot

Allow

You

In.

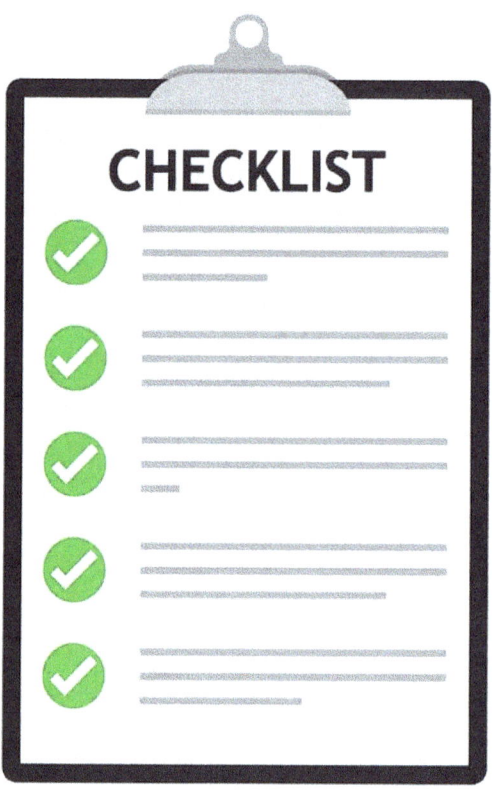

SHORT

Trying hard
                    Yet, still
Coming
Up short.

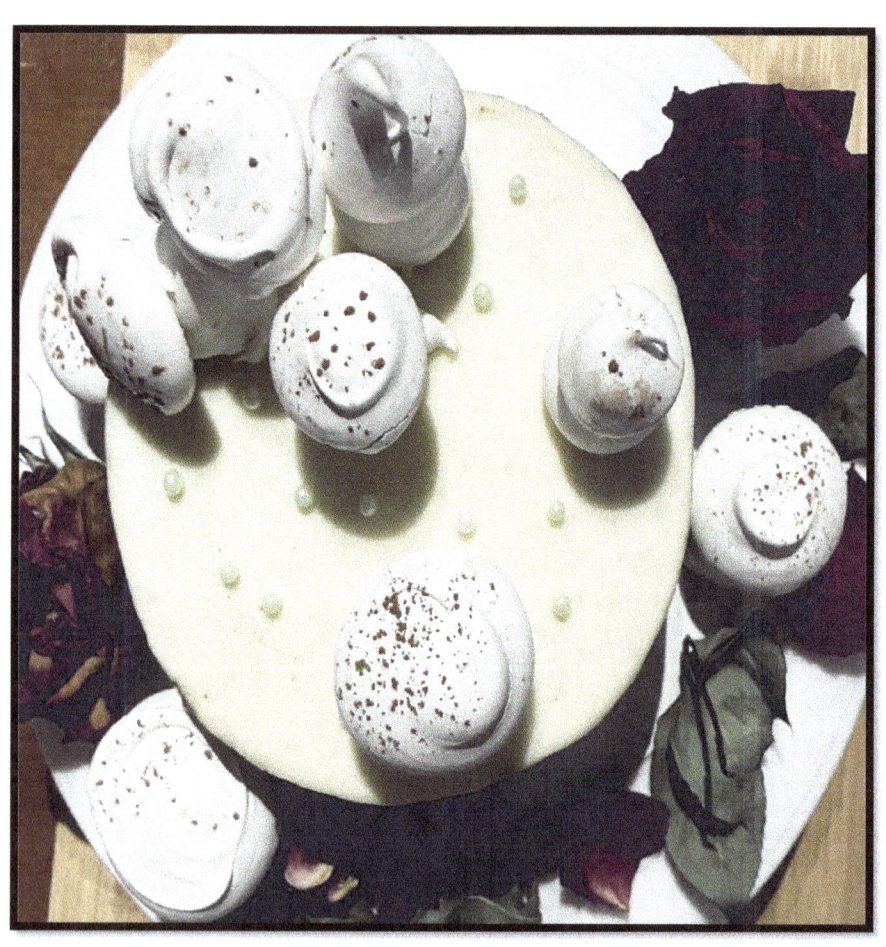

Practicing

HOVERING

The ceiling, stark

White

And naked.

Hovering

Over

The body

Waiting

For what

Feels

Like a long time.

Lauren Ferry

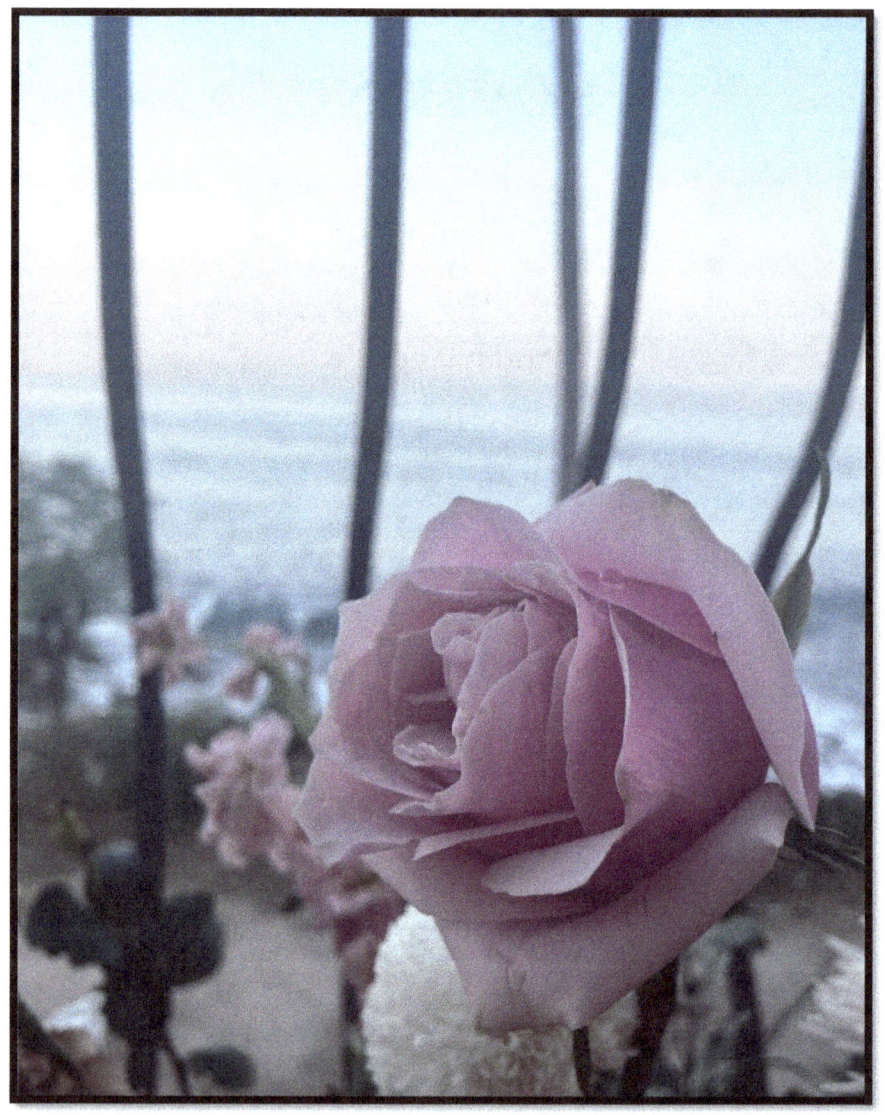

Mexico

A CLOVER FOR ME

A rose for you,

A clover for me.

Romance dances

Beneath.

Blood

Will drip

When thorns

Rise.

Run

Right over

My

Three

Leaves.

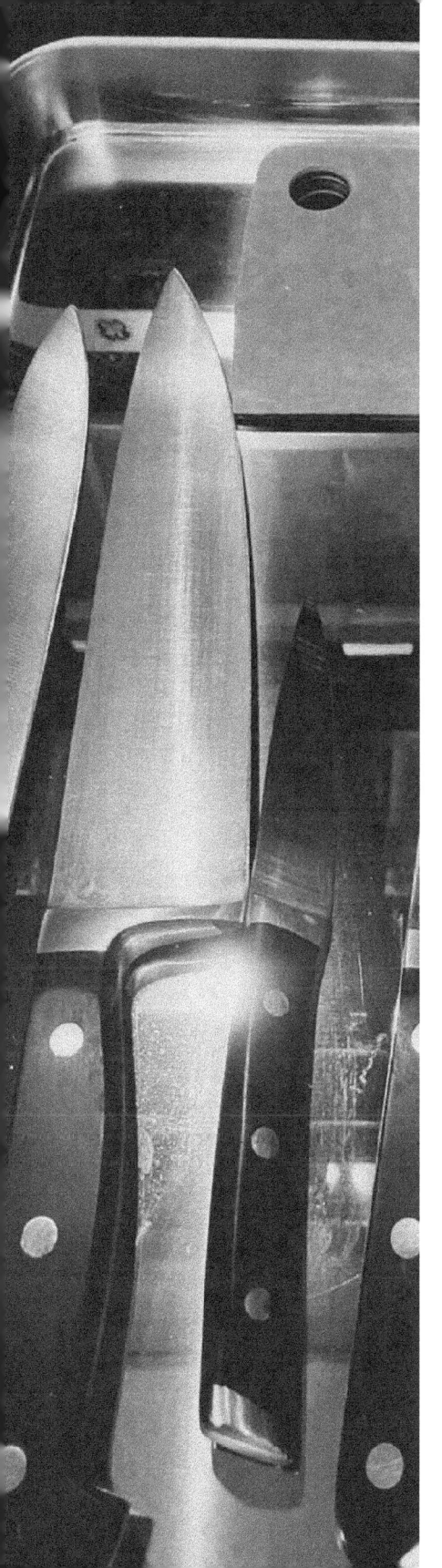

04

FOOD FOR THOUGHT

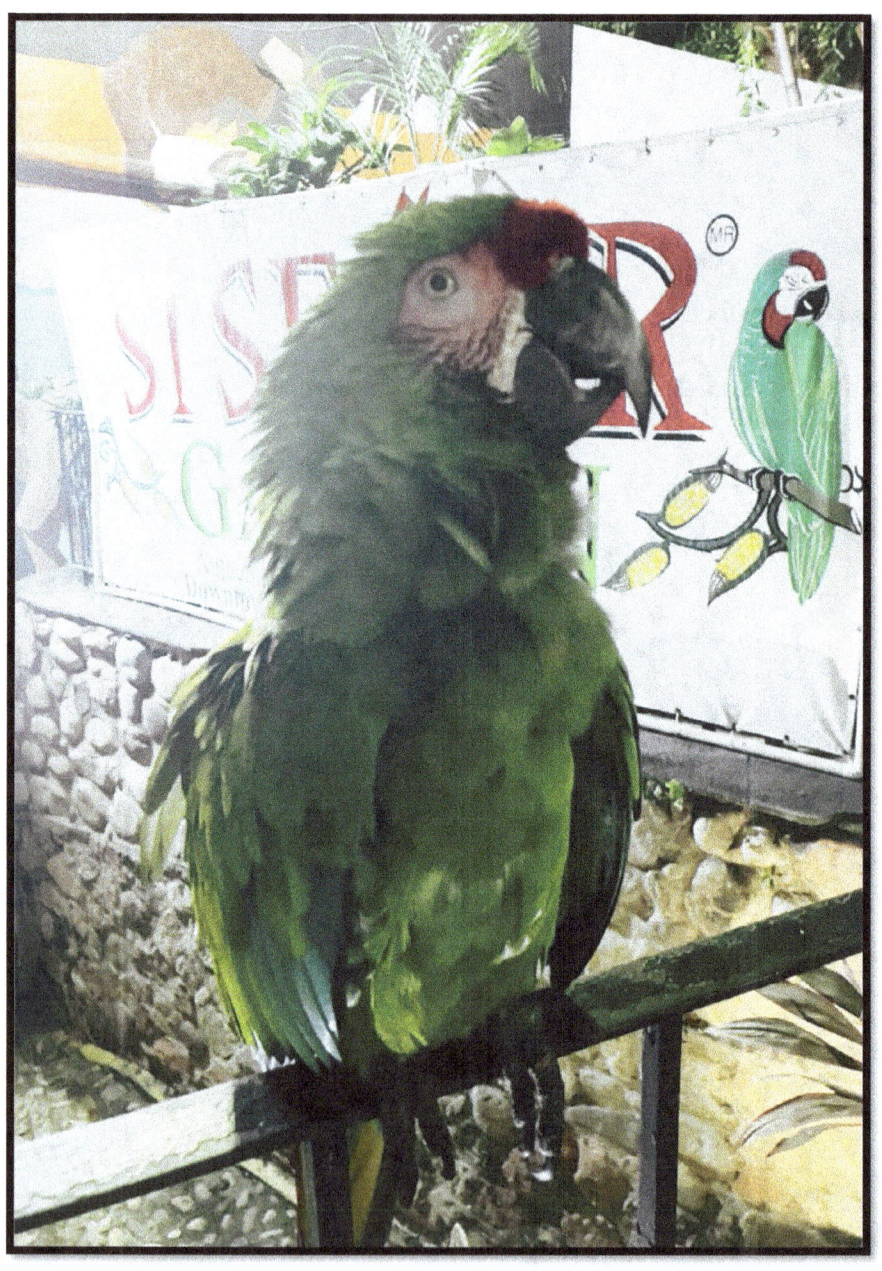

Mexico

THE BIRD SAID

"It's got nothing
To do
With me,"
The Bird said.
And she meant
It
When
She
Flew
Away
Narrowly.

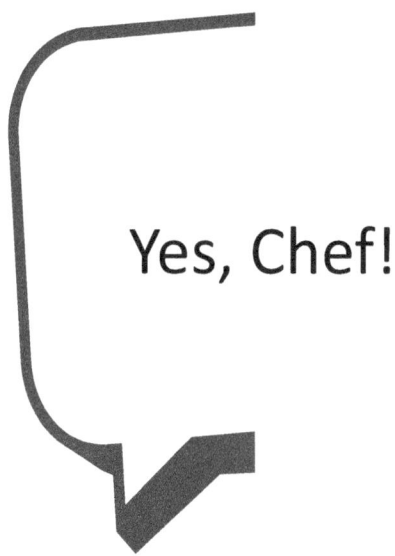

Yes, Chef!

SCORING

Scoring
The fat
Of the duck,
He said,
"It's better
to use a dull
Knife."

I contemplated
If it to be
True.

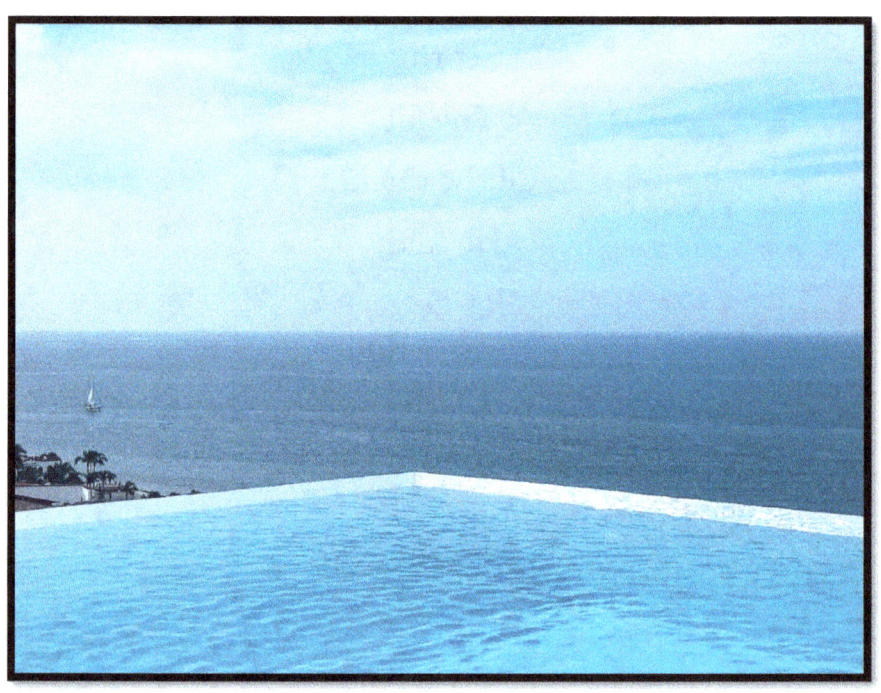

Casa Nawali Mexico

MY TURN

"It will

Not be,"

The Archangel said.

And it was finally my turn

To speak

So loudly

All

Worlds collided and collapsed

Quickly.

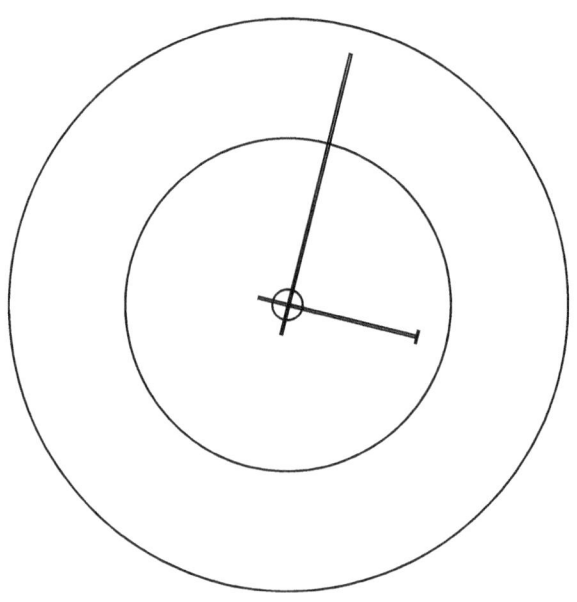

TIME

"Put it
To rest,"
He said.
And she knew
It was time.

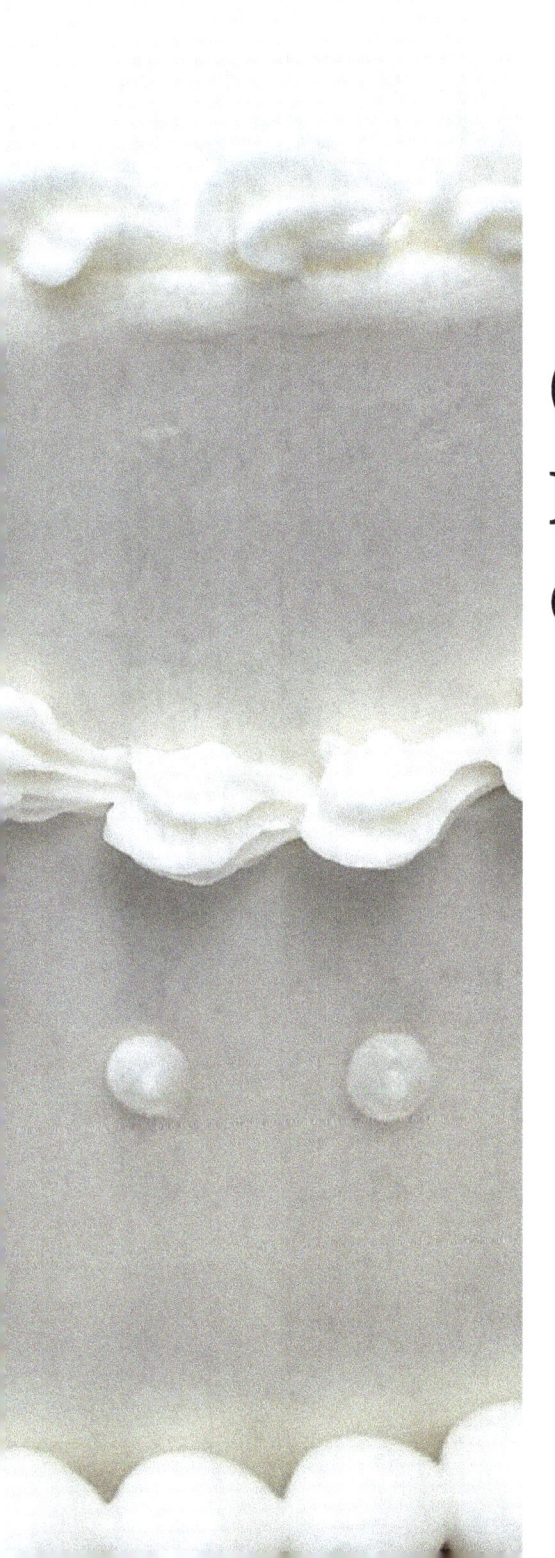

05
EATING
CAKE

Lauren Ferry

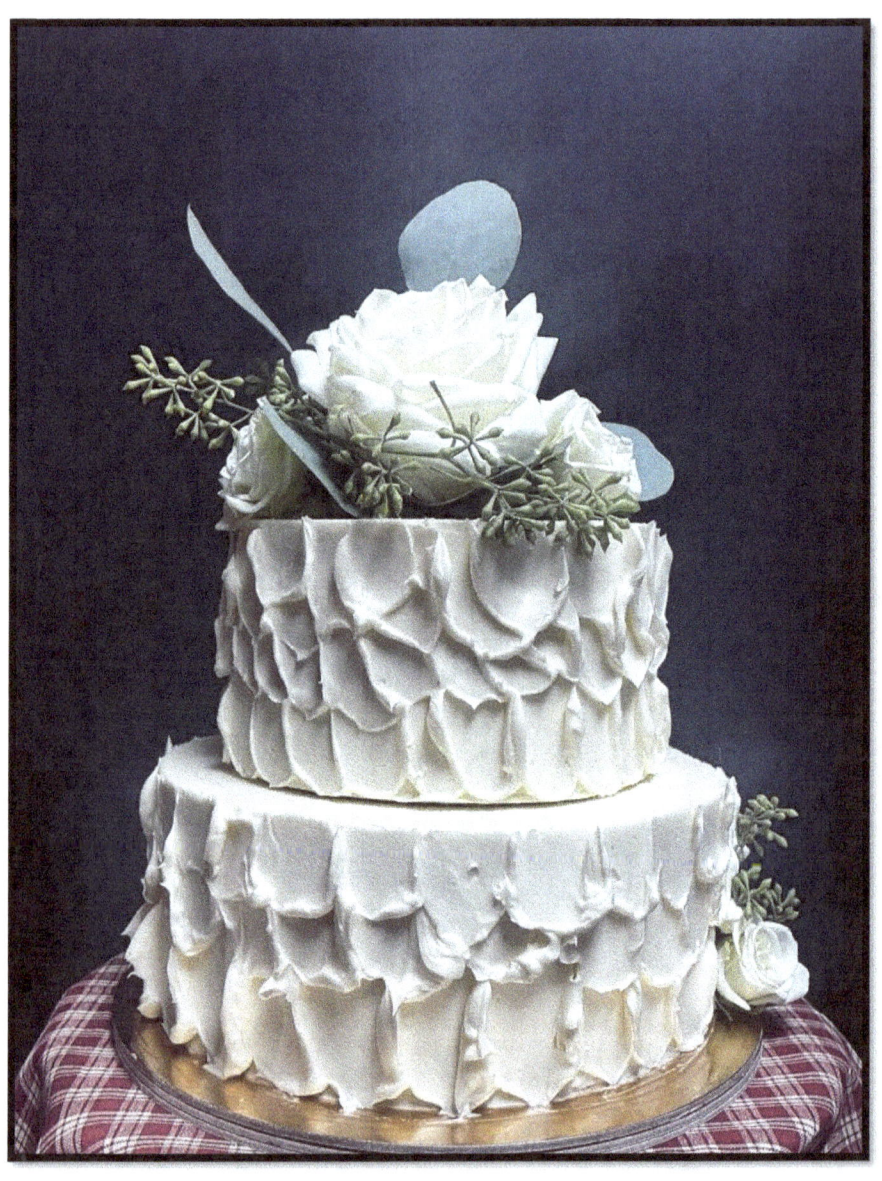

Geneva, Illinois Wedding

EATING CAKE

For the first

Time

In a long

Time

Stillness came.

I cannot be

Sure

What Marie ate,

But the cake

Was worth

The wait.

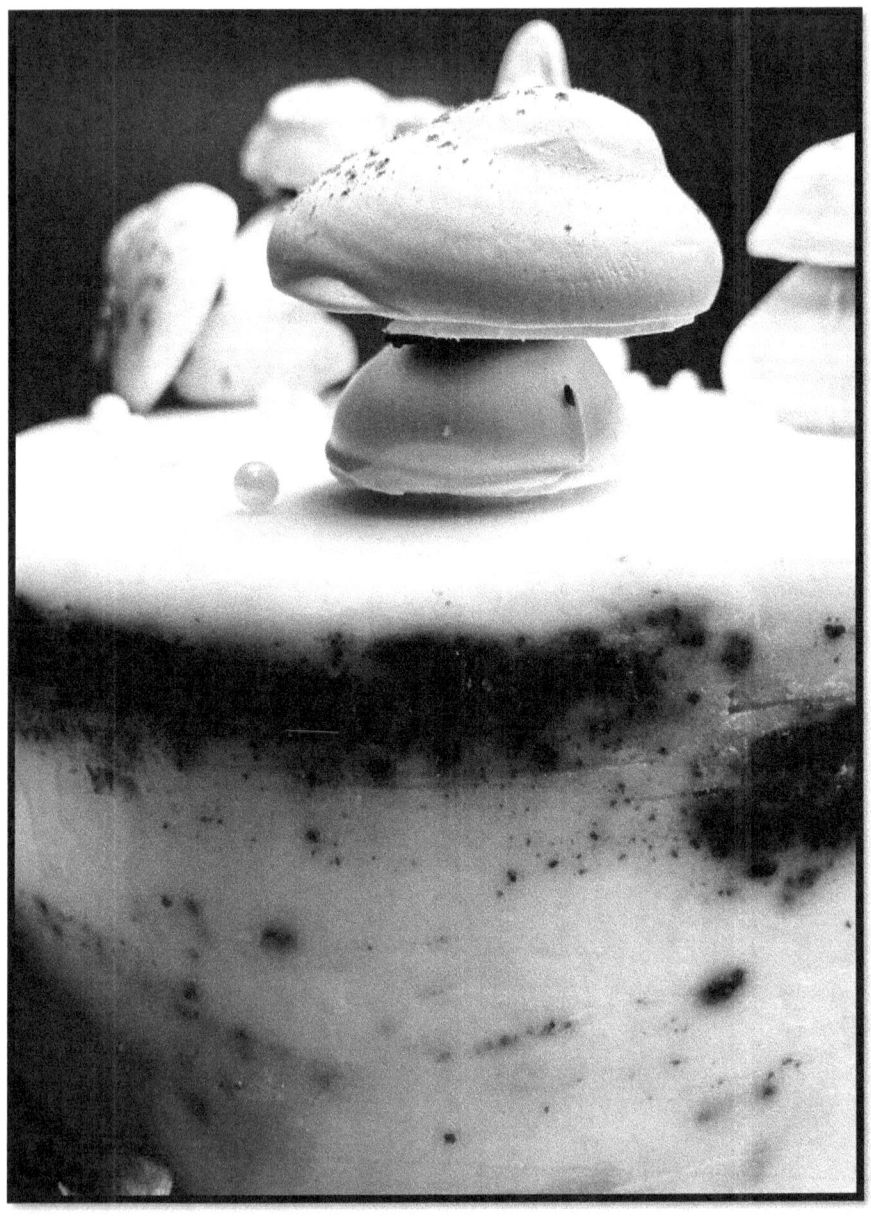

BUTTER CREAMING

Running a firm
Thirty-five degree
Angle,
The hardware spun
Like a carousel.
The cake spun
Round and round
Waiting
Around
For its smooth
Finish.

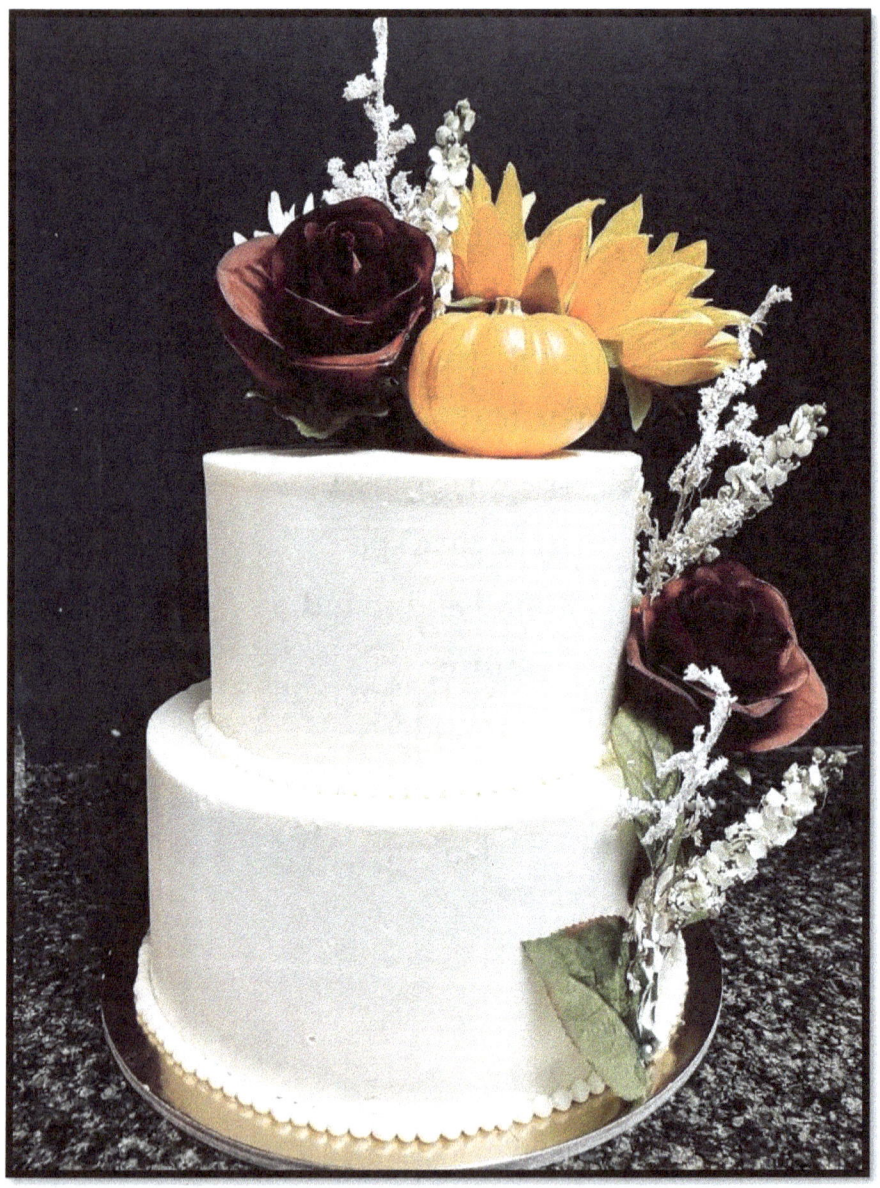

STIRRING AND SPILLING

The stirring

Comes,

S

P

I

L

L

S

When

You rise

To your own

Occasion.

ABOUT THE AUTHOR

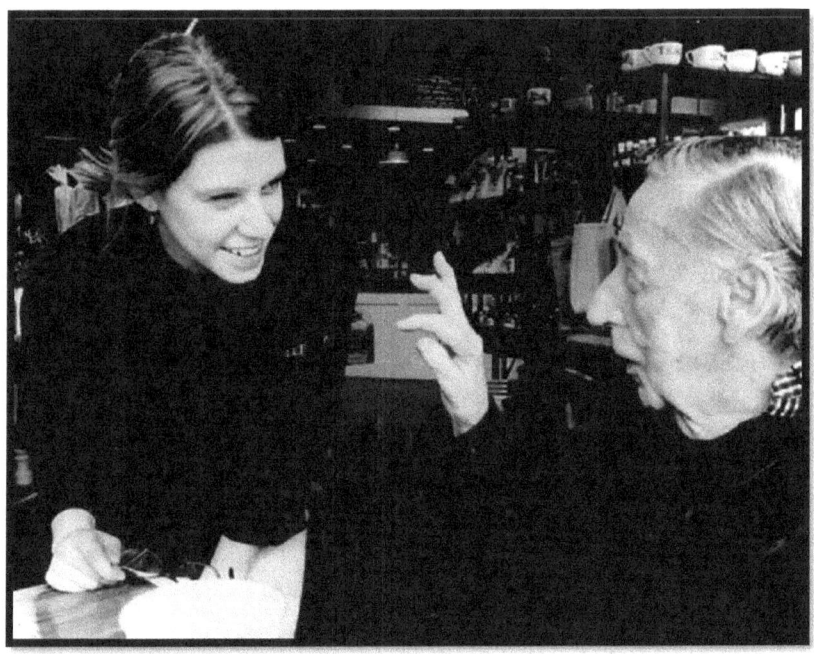

This one's for the cooks and my wonderful family!

A cook's life is not a glamorous life. This path will test you mentally and physically. I wrote this anthology of peculiar poems during my time working in a series of kitchens from Chicago to Napa Valley, California, including a Michelin star restaurant.

Today, I own a delivery bakery service called Ferry Cakes in Chicagoland.

Cheers!

Ferrybakescakes.com

www.ingramcontent.com/pod-product-compliance
Lightning Source LLC
Chambersburg PA
CBHW071230220526
45468CB00002B/797